ANCIENT ROME

Contents

1 Romulus and Remus

Now and Then Today, the city of Rome is the capital of a country called Italy. Two thousand years ago, Rome was the center of the world's greatest empire—the Roman's Empire. The Romans ruled all the lands around the Mediterranean Sea.

How did this great empire begin? The ancient Romans had a story, or **legend,** that explained how their city began.

Romulus and Remus

Mars, the Roman god of war, had twin sons named Romulus and Remus. When the twins were born, Mars promised that they would someday start a great empire.

A jealous uncle kidnapped the baby boys. He put them in a reed basket and threw the basket in the Tiber River. He thought the basket would fill with water and the babies would drown.

The twin boys were lucky. As the basket floated down the river, it drifted toward the riverbank. The basket hit the riverbank, and Romulus and Remus tumbled out. Then something moved in the bushes near the shore. It was a mother wolf.

She had heard the babies crying. She nudged them with her nose and touched them with her paw. The wolf knew right away that the twins were hungry, so she gave them milk along with her own cubs.

Later, a shepherd found the boys and raised them as his own sons. After the boys grew up, they decided to build a city near the Tiber River where the wolf had rescued them.

The brothers got into a fight over who would rule the city. During this fight, Romulus killed Remus. Romulus became the first king of the city that would be named after him—Rome.

This piece of art is made from very small pieces of tile. It shows Romulus, Remus, and the mother wolf.

Romulus ruled Rome for many years, until he mysteriously disappeared during a storm. The Romans believed that his father, the god Mars, took Romulus into heaven where he too became a god.

The Early Years

The story of Romulus and Remus is a legend. Legends usually are not true stories. Rome probably wasn't built near the Tiber River because a wolf rescued twins there. So what really happened?

Rome probably began when some farmers and shepherds built a village of small huts on one of the seven hills near the Tiber River. These people probably settled by the Tiber because it was a good place to live. The soil was rich. There was plenty of water and the river was good for travel.

The seven hills around the Tiber made it hard for enemies to approach. Rome grew as more people settled on those seven hills. That is why Rome became known as the "City of Seven Hills."

According to legend, Rome was founded in 753 B.C. The letters B.C. stand for "before Christ." That means that Rome was started 753 years before Jesus Christ was born, more than 2,750 years ago!

For many years, Rome was ruled by kings. But eventually the kings became too greedy for power. In 509 B.C. the Romans drove out their king. The Romans decided they did not trust anyone to be king. They made the city a republic, a kind of government in which people choose representatives to rule.

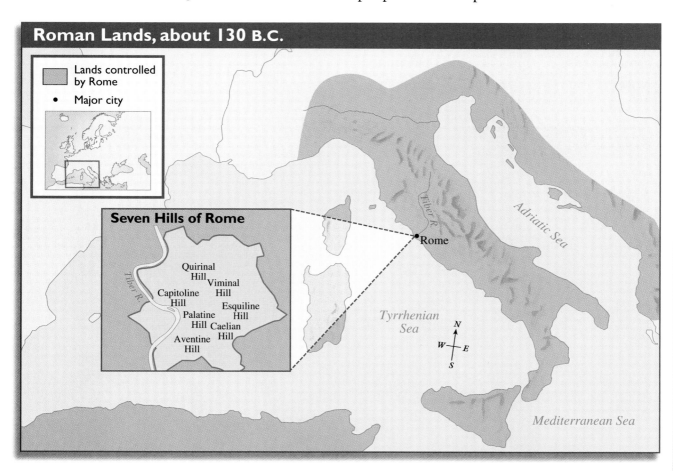

Roman Lands, about 130 B.C.

Lands controlled by Rome

• Major city

Seven Hills of Rome

Tiber R.

Quirinal Hill
Viminal Hill
Capitoline Hill
Esquiline Hill
Palatine Hill
Caelian Hill
Aventine Hill

Tiber R.

Rome

Adriatic Sea

Tyrrhenian Sea

N
W—E
S

Mediterranean Sea

Rome has been an important Italian city for more than 2,750 years.

2 Roman Gods and Goddesses

 **The Mighty Gods** The ancient Romans believed in many gods and goddesses. They believed that the gods controlled everything in nature: the wind, sun, rain, and even earthquakes.

The ancient Romans, like the ancient people of Greece, called Greeks, believed their gods interfered with almost everything humans did. The goddess Juno watched over Roman brides and their marriages. And Mars decided which side should win a battle or lose a war.

If a Roman farmer had a good crop, it was because the gods were pleased with him. If the same farmer had a bad crop, it was because the gods were angry with him. Because of this, the ancient Romans worried about angering their gods.

Keeping the Holy Fire Burning

Flavia was in a great hurry. She ran barefoot across the plowed fields of her family's farm. "Please, Vesta," she prayed, "please, let me get home in time, before the holy fire goes out. Why do I talk so much?" she asked herself. "Why can't I remember my duties?"

Flavia and her friend Meta had spent most of the morning washing clothes in a stream. They talked as they worked.

The Temple of Vesta was one of the many buildings in an area of Rome called the Forum.

Then, Flavia remembered that she had forgotten to keep the holy fire of the goddess Vesta burning at home. She left the wet clothes with Meta and ran home as fast as she could.

Flavia's mother usually kept Vesta's fire burning, but today her mother had gone to the market to sell vegetables. Although Flavia was only nine, as the oldest daughter, it was her job to keep the holy fire burning.

Vesta was the goddess who watched over the sacred altar fire of every Roman home, and the fire of Rome itself. The Romans made no statues of Vesta. Fire alone was her **symbol.** The Romans worshiped Vesta at every meal by throwing food into their fires.

Flavia burst into the house. She rushed to the fire; it was only a few glowing embers. Quickly but carefully, she placed some straw on the embers and blew gently to bring the flames back to life. Soon the fire burned brightly once again.

"Oh, thank you, Vesta," Flavia said, closing her eyes in prayer.

Very gently, Flavia placed some twigs on the burning straw. When the twigs were blazing, she put some charcoal in the fire. Flavia and her family believed that the scent of burning charcoal throughout the day and night meant that Vesta was keeping watch over the family.

This ornament shows the god Janus. Janus watched over doorways and archways everywhere in Rome.

Flavia and her family felt very close to Vesta and to the god Janus (JAY nuss), who also watched over Roman homes. Janus was a special god with two faces, one in the front of his head and one in the back. Janus had two faces so he could watch over the beginning and the end of all things. It was Janus who watched over every doorway of every building, keeping an eye on who came in and who went out.

Later Flavia thanked the gods that the holy flame had not died out. She would have dishonored her family if she had failed in her duty to keep the fire burning. She was very grateful that the gods had saved her from dishonor. She promised them she would never forget again.

vocabulary
symbol a picture or object that is a sign for something; for example, the American flag is a symbol of the United States

3 The Roman Republic

A **Boy Visits Rome** Lucius (LOO shee us) dressed in the dark. Everyone was asleep in his grandfather's villa, or country house—everyone except the kitchen slaves, who got up early every day to prepare the morning meal.

Lucius was about to try his luck driving a chariot. It was a children's chariot, towed by a goat instead of a horse, but he was still very excited.

Lucius ran barefoot over the stone floors of the villa. He carried his sandals until he reached a smooth path that ran between the statues and the fountain in the outer garden. He put on his sandals and went through the garden out to a long driveway.

Simon, a Greek slave who was Lucius's teacher and friend, waited by the chariot holding the long reins.

"Go slowly until you reach the road," Simon warned.

Lucius gripped the reins but barely stayed on as the chariot lurched forward. Immediately, the chariot began going full speed, with Simon running behind, shouting.

It was a wild ride, but Lucius eventually got the goat under control and guided the chariot in a large circle, back to the villa. There he saw Simon, looking embarrassed, and his father, looking angry.

"Your mother better not hear of this, boy!" said Lucius's father. "Simon, take this goat back to the field. Lucius, go back and find a warm cloak. We go to Rome today."

"Yes, Father," said Lucius, and he ran to find his cloak. Today he would ride in his father's chariot, too!

Patricians and Plebeians

Lucius was a patrician (puh TRIH shun). That meant that his family had great wealth and power. His grandfather was a Roman senator and his father was an army commander who had led a **legion** of more than 4,000 soldiers. The family villa was in the center of a large farm. The farm produced olive oil and wine for the nearby city of Rome. Hundreds of slaves worked on the farm.

Only a very few Roman families were patricians. These families were very powerful. They controlled the government and the army.

> **vocabulary**
> **legion** a unit or group of soldiers

Roman children, like all children, loved to copy what adults did.
This child's chariot was pulled by a farm animal.

Ordinary Roman citizens were called plebeians (pleh BEE uhnz). Most plebeians were poor working men and women.

For many years the patricians had almost all of the power in Rome. They guarded their power and gave very little to the plebeians. The plebeians could make some laws in their assembly, but the Senate, which had control of all the money the government spent, was controlled by the patricians. The Senate controlled all the people who worked for the government and everything the government did with other countries.

The citizens of Rome voted each year to elect two **consuls.** The consuls commanded the army and made sure laws were carried out. They also led meetings of the Senate.

When Rome went to war, the consuls sometimes chose a dictator, or person to lead the country. The dictator had the power to command everyone else to do what he said. The dictator's job was to make sure that Rome was protected and that the Roman army got whatever it needed to win a war. But dictators were allowed to run Rome for only six months.

Lucius and his father arrived in Rome shortly after sunrise. The city was quite empty at that hour. They walked together across the Forum, the great open area that was the center of Rome. In the corner of the Forum, they sat together and watched as the shops opened for the day and the Romans began to cross the Forum on their way to work.

vocabulary
consul the most important official in the Roman republic

Lucius Quinctius Cincinnatus

"Lucius, this great city was built by men of **virtue**," said his father. "These men served Rome because it was their duty. They wanted nothing for themselves. One of the greatest of these men was Lucius Quinctius Cincinnatus (sin sih NAY tus). You are named for this great man.

"Cincinnatus," Lucius's father continued, "had a small farm on the Tiber River not far from the city. One day, he was plowing his fields when messengers of the Senate came to him. They asked him to put on his **toga** and come with them to the Senate. Cincinnatus was covered with dirt from his work, but he put on his toga and crossed the Tiber to Rome.

"When Cincinnatus reached the city, the senators announced that he had been chosen as dictator. They told him that an enemy force had trapped the entire Roman army in a mountain pass. The army would be destroyed unless help arrived soon.

"Cincinnatus ordered every shop in the city to be closed. He ordered every man and boy in the city to gather in a field with their weapons. Everyone was given a job, and soon they were ready to march. Cincinnatus led this citizen army to the rescue.

"They saved the Roman army. The next day Cincinnatus returned to the Senate. He told the senators that the army had been saved. Then he returned to his farm and went back to work in the fields.

"This great Roman wanted nothing from Rome except a chance to do his duty. That is why I named you Lucius—so you would always remember your duty as a Roman."

vocabulary
virtue goodness
toga a loose robe worn by citizens of ancient Rome

This statue shows Roman senators wearing togas.

The Punic Wars 4

The Roman Army **In its early days, Rome was a small city with a small army. This army was made up of Roman citizens and included both patricians and plebeians. It was considered a great honor for a Roman to be in the army and defend the city of Rome.**

The Romans fought against some of their neighbors. When the Romans **conquered,** they took control of the land and people living there. The Roman army was very large and powerful. By the year 265 B.C., the Roman army had conquered most of the Italian **peninsula.**

The Punic Wars

In 264 B.C., the Romans went to war against Carthage. Carthage was a powerful nation located across the Mediterranean Sea on the coast of North Africa. (Today, the city of Tunis stands where Carthage once stood.)

There is a special name for these wars against the Carthaginians—the Punic Wars. In Latin, the language the Romans spoke, the word *Punicus* means "Carthaginian." So when we say Punic War, we are talking about a war between Rome and Carthage. Since Rome and Carthage went to war three times, these wars are called the First, Second, and Third Punic Wars.

vocabulary

conquer to win control of a land by attacking an enemy or fighting a war

peninsula a piece of land sticking out into a body of water

The First Punic War

The First Punic War was unlike any war the Romans had ever fought. Carthage was a rich nation with a large navy. When the First Punic War began, Carthage had 500 fighting ships, and Rome had no navy at all.

This artwork shows Roman soldiers in battle.

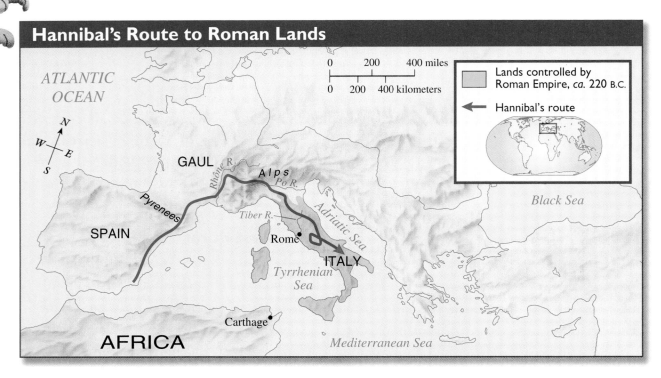

Hannibal's Route to Roman Lands

ATLANTIC OCEAN

GAUL

Rhone R.

Alps

Po R.

Pyrenees

SPAIN

Tiber R.

Rome

ITALY

Adriatic Sea

Black Sea

Tyrrhenian Sea

Carthage

AFRICA

Mediterranean Sea

0   200   400 miles

0   200   400 kilometers

Lands controlled by Roman Empire, *ca.* 220 B.C.

Hannibal's route

This map shows Hannibal's route from Spain to the lands of Rome.

The Romans were determined to win. They built warships and learned to fight at sea. They trained tens of thousands of sailors to man their warships. They fought the Carthaginians for 23 long years. When the first Punic War was over in 241 B.C., the Romans were the winners.

Hannibal

At the end of the First Punic War, a young boy was waiting for his father to return to Carthage. His father was a very important leader in the Carthaginian army. The little boy, whose name was Hannibal, wanted to be a soldier like his father, and, more than anything, he wanted to fight against the Romans.

When Hannibal's father returned, he was made commander of Carthage's army. He then conquered the rich lands along the northwest coast of the Mediterranean. Today this area is called Spain.

When he was nine years old, Hannibal went to Spain with his father and the army. Eventually Hannibal grew to be an excellent soldier, like his father. When he was 26 years old, he took command of the Carthaginian army.

Hannibal was a great general. He was brave and very clever in battle. He treated his men fairly and earned their respect and loyalty.

The Second Punic War

Hannibal still held a grudge against Rome. In 219 B.C., he attacked a town that was friendly with Rome. This attack started the Second Punic War.

Next, Hannibal made a very bold decision. He decided to march an army from Spain to Italy. This meant crossing wide rivers and the tall snow-covered mountains known as the Alps.

It would be hard enough for the soldiers to get across these rivers and mountains. But Hannibal also had to get thousands of horses and dozens of elephants across these barriers. The Carthaginian army used African elephants in battle. Most of their enemies in Europe had never seen elephants and were terrified by these giant animals.

The Romans thought that no army would ever be able to cross the rugged Alps. But they were wrong! It took 15 hard days, and Hannibal lost almost half his men, but the Carthaginians made it over the Alps and onto the Italian peninsula.

Hannibal fought the Romans on the Italian peninsula for the next 16 years. He won great battles, but he could not make the Romans give up.

Eventually, the Romans sent an army to attack Carthage. Hannibal rushed back home to protect the city from the Romans. Hannibal was defeated outside Carthage by a Roman army under the command of a general named Scipio Africanus (SIP ee oh af rih KAY nus).

Carthage surrendered, but Hannibal himself continued to fight. He moved from place to place, avoiding the Romans and joining their enemies. (In one attack he is said to have thrown big pots of snakes onto Roman ships!) When the Romans finally cornered him, Hannibal killed himself to avoid having to surrender to his longtime enemies.

The Third Punic War

After the Second Punic War, there was peace between Rome and Carthage for more than 50 years. But in 149 B.C., the Third Punic War began. The Romans sent a huge army to Africa. The fighting lasted only three years. In the end, the Romans destroyed the city of Carthage. The Carthaginians who were not killed were sold into slavery, and the Romans poured salt into the soil to make sure nobody could ever grow crops in Carthage again.

Hannibal and his soldiers, elephants, and horses are shown on this tapestry.

The Roman Army The Romans were expert conquerors. They had large, well-trained armies and their navy controlled the seas. After the Romans conquered an enemy, they made the conquered land part of Rome.

These lands were called **provinces.** The Roman Senate sent a governor to each of these areas. The governor made sure the province paid taxes to Rome. The Romans were not interested in starting a new government in every province. They usually let the conquered people keep their laws and customs. Sometimes they even made the conquered people citizens of Rome.

Greek Influences

The Romans conquered lands that had been ruled by the ancient Greeks. They brought many Greek statues and paintings back to Rome. They also brought Greek stories and plays, and Greek building styles.

The Romans copied the Greeks because they admired the beauty that the Greeks gave to what they painted and wrote and built.

The columns of Rome's Temple of Fortuna were copied from Greek architecture.

Wealthy Romans had Greek slaves who were teachers and doctors. Many Romans learned the Greek language. The Romans also brought Greek traditions and ways of living to the lands they conquered.

> **vocabulary**
> **province** an area under the control of a faraway government

Trouble in the Republic

As Rome conquered more lands, the wealthiest Romans grew richer. They bought slaves and land. When slaves did the farming, they were not paid. This meant that slave owners could sell crops for less than farmers who had to pay their workers. Poor people who did not have slaves soon lost their land, because they could not sell their crops and pay their workers.

Many of the people who had lost their land came to live in Rome. They were out of work and hungry. They wanted help from the Roman government. But the Roman government was controlled by the Senate, and many of the senators were wealthy landowners. These wealthy senators had little interest in helping the poor people of Rome.

Several leaders told the Senate that they must help those who had lost their land. The Senate did not listen to these men. The government of the Roman Republic had become very dishonest.

The age of the Roman Republic was nearly over. In its final days, one man took control of the government. His name was name was Julius Caesar (JOOL yus SEE zur).

Julius Caesar

Julius Caesar was born in 100 B.C. Although his parents were patricians, they were not wealthy, so Caesar knew he would have to work very hard to get ahead. As a young boy, he excelled in his studies.

Even as a young man, Caesar was an important figure in Rome.

He was also very good at sports, especially horseback riding.

Caesar served in the Roman army in Asia. Then he returned to Rome, where he worked as a lawyer. He made friends with many people in the Roman government. He wanted to work in the government, so he went to Greece to study public speaking.

Caesar became a great speaker and was elected to several jobs in the Roman government. One of those jobs was to conduct the games and shows for the city of Rome. Caesar borrowed lots of money from his wealthy friends. He spent the money to make the greatest games and shows in Roman history. Caesar's games and shows made him very popular with the people of Rome.

Caesar made friends with powerful leaders in the Senate and in the army. One of these friends was Pompey (PAHM pee), Rome's most famous general. Caesar also had enemies in the Senate, especially among the wealthy landowners.

Caesar was elected consul. Then he was named governor of two provinces that bordered the area the Romans called Gaul. Today we know this area as southern France and northern Italy.

The people of Gaul were fierce warriors. Soon Caesar was leading a large Roman army into Gaul. Caesar excelled as a general. He was a fine leader of his soldiers and a hero to the people of Rome.

Crossing the Rubicon

Caesar's old friend Pompey became very jealous of Caesar. He watched Caesar grow more powerful with each conquest in Gaul. Soon Pompey was no longer Rome's most famous general—Caesar was.

Pompey joined Caesar's enemies in the Senate. They hated and feared Caesar. He was too popular with the Roman people. His army had grown too powerful. They ordered Caesar to give up his army and return to Rome.

Caesar led his great army to the Rubicon (ROO bih kahn) River, which was the border between Gaul and Italy. Caesar stopped and thought about what he should do.

If his army crossed the Rubicon, he would be at war with Rome. But if he left his army in Gaul, he would have no defense against his enemies and they would probably kill him.

Caesar decided to fight. He led the army across the Rubicon and started a **civil war.**

vocabulary
civil war a war between people who live in the same country

Civil War

The war against Caesar did not go well for Pompey and Caesar's other enemies in the Senate. Caesar kept attacking until he drove his enemies out of Italy to Spain. He fought them in Spain and defeated them. From Spain he chased them to Greece, where he defeated them again. After this battle, Caesar generously forgave the senators who had fought against him.

Pompey himself escaped to Egypt. But when he landed in Egypt, the king of Egypt had him killed. This proved to be a terrible mistake.

According to legend, Caesar saw the goddess Roma on the banks of the Rubicon. She asked him not to invade his own country, but he decided to go against her advice.

Arrival in Egypt In 48 B.C., Julius Caesar arrived in Alexandria, Egypt, with a small group of soldiers. Caesar and his men were looking for Pompey. They went to the king's palace. The king, who was only 13 years old, gave Caesar a gift—Pompey's head.

The king of Egypt had trusted his advisers. They had promised him that Caesar would be happy to learn that Pompey was dead. They were wrong. Pompey was a Roman general. Caesar saw the murder of Pompey as an insult to Rome.

Cleopatra

While Caesar was still a guest at the palace, a servant entered carrying a large, rolled-up rug. He took it into Caesar's private chamber and carefully lowered it to the floor.

Caesar watched as the rug was unrolled and a beautiful woman appeared. She said her name was Cleopatra (klee oh PAT ruh), and she was the queen of Egypt.

Cleopatra begged Caesar to protect her from her brother, the king. She said the king and his advisers were planning to murder her.

It took a little while for Caesar to reply. He had been staring at Cleopatra and listening to her voice. He would certainly protect her. He wanted to keep her near. Cleopatra stayed with Caesar.

The king and his advisers were angry that Cleopatra had outsmarted them. They were also angry that Caesar had offered his protection to Cleopatra. They ordered the Egyptian army to surround the palace. They thought this would make Caesar change his mind about protecting Cleopatra. Once again, they were wrong.

Notice Cleopatra's clothing and jewelry in this carving.

Caesar ordered the Roman army in nearby Syria to march on Alexandria. Caesar killed the king's chief adviser and forced the king to escape from his own palace. When the Roman army arrived, Caesar took command. He easily defeated the Egyptian army. The king of Egypt died in the battle.

Cleopatra was very grateful to Caesar. She asked him to travel through Egypt with her. They sailed up the Nile River on her royal **barge.** Caesar learned a lot about Cleopatra on this journey.

Cleopatra was actually Greek, not Egyptian. The Greek king Alexander the Great had conquered Egypt and built the great city of Alexandria. Cleopatra was a descendant of one of Alexander's Greek generals.

Cleopatra had worked hard preparing herself to be a good ruler. She learned about other countries from people who came to study in Alexandria's great library. She also learned to speak many languages.

She was the only one in the history of her royal family who could speak to the Egyptian people in their own language.

As they traveled up the Nile, Cleopatra showed Caesar the wonders of the ancient world. By the end of their journey, Caesar trusted Cleopatra. He did not want to make Egypt a Roman province. He wanted Cleopatra to remain queen of Egypt. Caesar also began a romance with Cleopatra.

Caesar, however, was a busy man. He left Egypt to finish the war against Pompey's remaining forces.

This tall structure, called an obelisk, *is known as "Cleopatra's needle." It was built in Alexandria, Egypt.*

More Conquests Julius Caesar continued to conquer. When he left Egypt, he led his army to Asia Minor, the home of modern-day Turkey. There, as always, Caesar excelled as a general.

His message to the Senate about his latest conquest was only three Latin words: *"Veni, vidi, vici"* (VEE nee VEE dee VEE kee), which means, "I came, I saw, I conquered."

Next, Caesar went to North Africa and won a great victory. Then, he went to Spain and defeated forces led by the sons of Pompey. Finally, he returned to Rome, where he became dictator of Rome and the most powerful man in the world.

Caesar made changes in the Roman government. He lowered taxes, appointed new senators, and replaced several greedy governors in the provinces. He gave land to Roman soldiers and food to the poor.

Caesar's enemies in the Senate did not like these changes. They thought Caesar was acting like a king.

Caesar invited Cleopatra to Rome to celebrate his victories. He gave her gifts and placed a statue of her in a temple.

Caesar's enemies in the Senate worried that Caesar would marry Cleopatra and move the government to Alexandria. They also disliked the way Caesar had destroyed the republic and set himself up as a permanent dictator. They decided to kill Caesar.

The Assassination

On March 15, 44 B.C., several of Caesar's enemies entered the Senate chamber with knives hidden under their togas.

Caesar speaks to members of the Roman Senate.

This painting shows the murder of Caesar.
It was painted by the Italian artist Vincenzo Camuccini in 1793.

When Caesar entered the Senate, his enemies drew their knives and stabbed him. One of the attackers was Brutus (BROO tus), a man Caesar had forgiven after Pompey's defeat. Caesar considered Brutus a friend and was surprised that Brutus had joined the murderers. His last words before he died were *"Et tu, Brute?"* or "You too, Brutus?"

Marc Antony and Octavian

After Caesar died, another civil war began. On one side were Brutus and other men who supported the killing of Caesar. On the other side were the supporters and friends of Caesar. In 42 B.C., Caesar's friends won the war. The leaders of this group were Marc Antony and Octavian.

Marc Antony was a famous general. He wore a thick cloak that looked like a lion's skin.

He told his soldiers that he was related to the legendary hero Hercules, who had killed a mighty lion and worn its skin as a cloak. Antony's soldiers respected his courage in battle, but Antony could be boastful and, at times, reckless.

Marc Antony shared control of the government with Caesar's adopted son, Octavian (ahk TAY vee un). Octavian called himself "the young Caesar." He was only 18 years old when Caesar died. Octavian was the opposite of Antony. He was very proper in his dress and his manner and very careful and cautious about his decisions.

Antony and Octavian each took part of the Mediterranean world to command. Octavian's part was in the west, near Spain. Antony's part was in the east, near Egypt. They shared control of the Italian peninsula.

Antony and Cleopatra

Antony wanted to conquer more lands in the east, but he needed money for his army. He asked Cleopatra to trade the riches of Egypt for his protection. Cleopatra agreed. She invited Antony to stay with her in Egypt and the two fell in love.

Antony's wife died soon after. Though he was free to marry Cleopatra, Antony would not. He understood that many important Roman men did not trust Cleopatra. She was too clever, too rich, and too powerful. She was a foreigner and, worst of all, she was a woman.

This wall sculpture shows a warship like the ones Octavian used.

Antony left Cleopatra, returned to Rome, and married Octavian's sister, Octavia. He knew that the important Roman men would approve of this marriage, and he figured the marriage would help him keep the peace with Octavian. Despite this marriage, Antony returned to the east three years later. He went back to his wars of conquest—and to Cleopatra.

Things went badly in Antony's wars. He lost half his army and conquered nothing. The army needed food, clothing, and weapons.

Octavia wanted to help her husband. She loaded ships with supplies and sailed to the east. Antony refused Octavia's help. He ordered her to return to Rome. Antony made it clear to everyone in Rome that he preferred Cleopatra to his noble Roman wife.

Octavian was angry because Antony had insulted and embarrassed his sister. He spoke out against Antony and Cleopatra. He said they were planning to take control of the entire Roman world.

Octavian prepared for war against Antony and Cleopatra. As always, he was careful. He asked Agrippa, Rome's most famous naval commander, to help.

Octavian attacked first. Agrippa trapped Antony and Cleopatra and forced them to fight at sea, where they were no match for Agrippa. The defeated couple escaped to Egypt.

The end came quickly. Antony's army surrendered. Antony killed himself. Cleopatra knew that Octavian would bring her back to Rome in chains. She dressed in her most beautiful costume and held a deadly snake to her skin. When Octavian's guards found her, Cleopatra appeared to be asleep, but she was dead.

Octavian's Return When Octavian returned to Rome, he was 33 years old. Up to that time he had a remarkable life. He had been adopted by Julius Caesar as a boy and named consul of Rome when he was only 19 years old.

Octavian and Marc Antony had defeated Caesar's enemies and had each taken a part of the Roman world to command. Then Octavian had defeated Antony and Cleopatra. He had conquered Egypt and taken Cleopatra's treasure for himself. Along with all his wealth, he had 280,000 soldiers in his army.

Octavian was ready to begin the most important part of his life. For the rest of his life, Octavian was to lead Rome. He would rule with intelligence and wisdom.

Closing the Doors of War

Octavian showed his wisdom shortly after he returned from Egypt. The Roman people were celebrating Octavian's victory, which ended the civil war and saved Rome. Octavian led a great crowd to the temple of Janus. The gates of this temple were left open during times of war and closed during peacetime. Since Rome was almost always at war, the gates had been closed only twice in hundreds of years.

When the gates of the temple of Janus were closed, Rome was at peace.

Octavian closed the gates. By doing this, he was telling the Roman people they would now live in peace. He was also telling the Roman Senate that he could be trusted to protect Rome.

Soon afterward, Octavian bought land for his soldiers. He told them it was time to leave the army and go back to being farmers.

Octavian himself went back to his job as consul. He was re-elected three years in a row. After he was re-elected he told the Senate he wanted to give back all his power. He wanted to serve Rome in any way the Senate decided.

Octavian Becomes Augustus

The Senate decided that Octavian should command the armies in all the large provinces. They also decided that Octavian should have a new name. He was to be called Augustus (awe GUS tus) Caesar. *Augustus* is a Latin word that means the "revered one" or the most admired and respected.

Augustus was to be the First Citizen of Rome, and the month of his birth would be renamed for him. Today, we call that month August. (July had been named for Julius Caesar a few years earlier.)

Augustus was not a king or a dictator. All his power came from the Senate. He was always very respectful to the senators and the assemblies. The senators trusted Augustus, because he used his power wisely.

Augustus used his power to change the government. He named new governors for the provinces and new senators for the Senate.

He made changes in the Roman army. He paid soldiers more money and made the army a good place for poor men to earn a living.

Augustus built good roads throughout the Roman world. These roads connected Rome and the provinces. Augustus often visited the provinces to check if the governors were doing a good job.

Augustus Rebuilds Rome

At the end of the civil war, Rome was a dirty, overcrowded city. Most of the streets and buildings needed repairs. The aqueducts, which carried water to the city, were also crumbling.

Many people who had lost their land during the civil war were now living in Rome. These people were poor and hungry. They lived in crumbling old buildings that often caught fire or collapsed.

Augustus bought food for the poor. He rebuilt many crumbling buildings. He made safe building laws and started Rome's first fire and police departments. He put Agrippa, his great naval commander, in charge of the city's water supply. Agrippa and his men rebuilt the old aqueducts.

Augustus wanted everyone to know about the many citizens who had helped to make Rome great. He placed many statues of Roman heroes around a beautiful new Forum, which he built for the Roman people.

Augustus filled the city with beautiful new buildings. He built theaters, meeting places, and a grand new Senate building.

This statue of Augustus was discovered at Primaporta, near Rome.

The beautiful Pantheon was used to worship all of the Roman gods. It was built during the rule of Augustus.

Augustus changed Rome from a dirty, ugly place to one of the most beautiful cities in the world.

Augustus also strengthened Roman religion. He repaired all the old temples in the city and built new ones. He brought back many old religious ceremonies and festivals.

Augustus loved books and ideas. He often visited with writers and poets to listen as they read their work aloud. He urged wealthy Romans to be patrons to writers. These patrons gave money to writers so they could keep writing. During the time of Augustus, talented writers wrote many great works, including several that are still read today.

Rome's First Emperor

Rome honored Augustus for rebuilding the city and making life better for the people. They named him "Father of His Country." He would later be called Rome's first emperor.

Although Augustus was the most powerful man in the world, his way of life was simple. His house was small. His meals were plain. He was devoted to his wife and family and the people of Rome.

Augustus ruled Rome for 45 years, until A.D. 14. The letters A.D. stand for the Latin words *anno Domini,* which mean "in the year of the Lord." This tells about how many years have passed since the birth of Jesus.

The Roman World The Roman world was once very easy to see. If you wanted to see everything Roman in 750 B.C., all you had to do was climb a hill near the Tiber River. You would see a few farms, fishermen's huts, and small clusters of houses.

The Roman world grew as the years passed. As you know from reading the earlier lessons, the Romans were good at conquering other lands. They were also good at ruling places far from Rome. The Romans were expert at protecting conquered peoples so they could work hard and send taxes to Rome.

Eventually, the Roman world grew so large that the only way to see everything Roman would have been from a satellite high above Earth. But of course there were no satellites back in those days. The Romans used maps to show all the provinces they ruled. These Roman provinces were located on three continents: Europe, Asia, and Africa. So their map had to be pretty large.

Take a look at the map below. It shows the Roman Empire when it was very large. Let's take a quick tour of the empire!

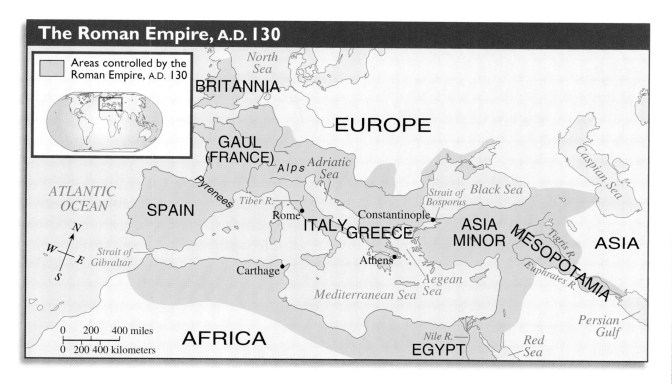

Rome's empire spread from the Italian peninsula through most of Europe, and parts of Asia and Africa.

Italy and the Mediterranean

The city of Rome itself is located on the Italian peninsula, near the center of the map. Do you see it? If you can't find the Italian peninsula, look for the piece of land that looks a lot like a boot. Can you see the toe and the high heel?

The Italian peninsula is part of the European continent. Between the Italian peninsula and rest of Europe are the Alps, a high snow-covered mountain range. These are the mountains that Hannibal and his elephants crossed during the Second Punic War.

The Italian peninsula sticks out into the Mediterranean Sea. Once the Romans had conquered the Italian peninsula, they began to expand their empire to include islands and coastal areas in the Mediterranean. After a while, the Romans controlled the whole Mediterranean region. They even started calling the Mediterranean "our sea"!

Greece and the Balkans

The Adriatic Sea is northeast of the Italian peninsula. Just across the Adriatic Sea to the east is Greece. As you know, ancient Greece was a very important place for the Romans. The Romans learned many things from the Greeks. They brought Greek ideas about education, art, building, and government back to Rome and spread these ideas to the other lands they conquered.

To the east of Greece is the Aegean Sea, which is connected to another large body of water called the Black Sea.

The narrow waterway, or strait, that connects these two seas is called the Strait of Bosporus.

The city of Constantinople is located near the Strait of Bosporus. (On modern maps Constantinople is called Istanbul, and today it is the capital of Turkey.) This ancient city was very important to the Roman Empire. You will learn more about it later.

Asia and Africa

To the east of Constantinople is the peninsula known as Asia Minor. Today it is the home of part of the modern nation of Turkey, but two thousand years ago it was part of the Roman Empire. Julius Caesar was in Asia Minor when he sent his famous *Veni, vidi, vici* message.

The Romans also controlled the ancient land of Mesopotamia and the great kingdom of Egypt. Egypt was the home of Cleopatra and was one of the richest of the Roman provinces.

The remains of the Library of Ephesus, in Turkey, show the influence of ancient Rome.

It had ports on the Mediterranean Sea and the Red Sea, as well as rich lands along the great Nile River.

The Romans also had provinces scattered all along the coast of North Africa. Part of that long coastline was controlled by Carthage up until the end of the Third Punic War, when the Romans plowed the soil with salt.

Back to Europe

At the western end of that long North African coastline is the Strait of Gibraltar. This strait connects the Mediterranean Sea with the Atlantic Ocean. Spain is north of the Strait of Gibraltar, on the continent of Europe. The Romans conquered Spain and, with the help of Julius Caesar, the large area to the north, which they called Gaul. Today, we know this area as France.

The Romans also had an island province north of the European continent, which they called Britannia. Today this land is part of Great Britain.

All Roads Lead to Rome

When you control such a large empire, you have to have some way of getting from place to place. The Romans solved this problem by building excellent roads. These roads were paved with smooth slabs of stone. The Roman army could travel quickly over the paving stones and go wherever it was needed.

There were more than 50,000 miles of such roads in the Roman Empire. These roads connected all the provinces of the Roman Empire to Rome itself. That is why the Romans used to say that "all roads lead to Rome."

Today, in areas of Asia, Africa, and Europe, highways and railroad lines still follow the ancient routes of the Roman roads.

The Appian Way, the most famous road of ancient Rome, was built in 312 B.C. Parts of the road are still used today.

Grandfather's Traveling School One morning in A.D. 100, a Roman patrician named Marcus heard the slap of small sandals echoing off the stone floor of his villa. Marcus wondered which of his children was up so early.

The slapping sound grew louder, and Marcus saw Linus, his seven-year-old son, carrying a great armload of scrolls. Marcus called out in a loud whisper, but Linus didn't hear him.

At that moment, the footsteps were interrupted by an awful crash followed by the sound of heavy scrolls bouncing and rolling on the smooth stone floor.

Marcus hurried out into the hall. Linus was trying to gather up the scrolls. Lucia, his eleven-year-old sister, was shaking her head and scolding her brother.

"Now you have woken Father. Why can't you be careful? Next you will wake Grandfather."

She was right. The head of the family was awake and shouting at his grandson.

"You won't find answers in those scrolls, boy. You and your sister have a lot to learn, and you won't learn it crawling around my villa in the dark. Tell Nikos, your teacher, that we are going to Rome. But first, I'll have a word with my son."

Marcus smiled at his father as the senator led them outside.

"Marcus, my grandchildren have been in the countryside too long. I asked them some questions yesterday. They know almost nothing about Rome. They have never even seen an aqueduct! It is time they learned, and as head of this family, I'm going to see to it. They'll be in my traveling school beginning today."

Marcus was grateful to his father, who was a Roman senator. He knew he would be giving Linus and Lucia a wonderful gift.

Linus and Lucia climbed aboard a large wagon. Nikos the teacher was next, followed by two slaves who would cook meals and care for the horses.

The senator wore a purple-trimmed toga and rode a beautiful black horse. He waved good-bye to Marcus and rode away, followed by his guards and the heavy wagon.

They rode a while on the main road. Then Grandfather turned down a smaller road. Soon they saw a great cloud of dust ahead. Grandfather rode back to the wagon.

Road Building

"Linus and Lucia, you are going to learn how to build a road," said Grandfather. "Climb down. We'll walk from here."

As they neared the dust cloud, they saw hundreds of men digging and carrying stones.

Their grandfather explained: "First these men dig a trench—a big hole in the ground—and lay large stones and gravel. Then they lay down smooth slabs of stone to make the road's surface. They also make the road a little higher in the middle so that water will flow off it.

"Nikos will show you a map of the Roman roads, which connect all the Roman provinces. These fine roads are one of our most valuable treasures.

"Next," Grandfather continued, "we're going to see where this road is going. We will have a good view from that hilltop."

Bridge Building

The view was very good indeed. The road was headed across a broad valley toward a wide river. Hundreds of men were building a bridge across the river.

Again, the senator explained how it was done. "First, they lined two boats up side by side. Then they built a wooden platform across them. They added more boats and made the platform longer until it finally went all the way across the river.

"When the long platform was finished, they began building the underwater **pillars** to support the bridge.

> **vocabulary**
> **pillar** a tall, solid support post

In ancient Rome, there were no books. People read information on scrolls, long sheets rolled around sticks.

This Roman aqueduct was built during the time of Emperor Trajan, who ruled from A.D. 98 – A.D. 117.

"They pounded a wooden stake into the bottom of the river. Then another stake next to it, and another, until they made a circle of stakes. They pulled chains around the circle of stakes to make the circle very tight, so water would not leak in between the stakes.

"When the chains were tight, they emptied out the water inside the circle. Then they built a stone pillar in the empty circle of stakes. They built all the pillars the same height and then connected them with wooden arches.

"Next they will build another platform over the arches. Then they will replace the wooden arches and the wooden platform with stone to finish the bridge. This stone bridge will soon be strong enough to hold a Roman army legion."

Aqueducts

Linus and Lucia's grandfather pointed in the other direction. "Look up the valley to those hills. Do you see what is between them?" he asked.

"I do," replied Lucia. "It looks like a bridge, but it is so much larger and so high in the air. It connects the tops of those two hills. What is it, Grandfather?"

"It is an aqueduct, and it carries water from the mountain lakes to the city of Rome. The aqueduct is a great pipe for the water to flow high in the air over valleys and hillsides.

"Aqueducts are built like bridges from arches of stone connecting stone support pillars. The great pipe lies on top of the arches the way the road lies on the arches of the bridge."

A Visit to Rome Nikos smiled as he lifted the heavy scroll back into its case. Linus and Lucia had worked many hours learning the map of Roman roads. Their grandfather asked some hard questions about the map, but Linus and Lucia knew the answers.

That night they traveled to Rome. The smooth paved road was bright in the moonlight. The senator and his guards rode close to the wagon. The rumbling of the wagon and the clopping sounds of the horses' hooves filled the cool night air.

When they reached Rome, they found its narrow streets crowded with wagons. Although many Romans stayed in at night, food and supplies for the morning arrived while they slept.

They passed through noisy, crowded neighborhoods filled with apartment houses. The city grew quieter as they rode into the senator's neighborhood. And once they went though his house gates, the senator's gardens were as quiet as his country villa.

Slaves with torches ran out into the yard. They unloaded the wagon and led the horses to the stables.

The children followed their grandfather into the house. Then came Nikos, carrying his case of scrolls.

"Nikos, come and have some wine," said the senator. "The children did well with their lessons."

This painting was made on a wall of a house in Pompeii, Italy, around 50 B.C.

This picture shows the ruins of the Temple of Jupiter.

Tomorrow I want you to take Linus to the marketplaces of the city. That boy thinks that Rome is nothing but chariot races and gladiators. I want him to learn about life in our city, and he will find plenty of life in the marketplaces."

The Temple of Jupiter

Lucia woke up in a strange room. For a moment, she forgot she was in her grandfather's house in Rome. Then she jumped out of bed. Last night, Grandfather had promised a surprise if she got up early.

Lucia found him waiting near a stairway. The senator led the way up the stairs to the roof. Lucia took his hand as they went up the stairs.

When she looked up, she saw a strange light above the house. When they reached the top of the stairs, Lucia saw the source of the glowing light.

The first faint light of dawn had just reached a nearby hilltop. There, a huge white building glowed in the early light. On its roof stood an immense statue of a giant bearded man driving a chariot pulled by four great horses.

Grand pillars of pure white marble surrounded the entire building. Lucia had never seen anything as beautiful as that great white building.

"There is the greatest symbol of Rome, the Temple of Jupiter," Grandfather said. "Today we will visit that temple, just the two of us. Linus will go with Nikos to explore the marketplaces."

Lucia looked over the senator's gardens. The first birds began to sing. She saw Nikos and Linus leaving the house.

The Marketplace

"Nikos, are you sure we will see fish bigger than me?" asked Linus.

"Yes, Linus, and fish smaller than your fingers. We will see every fish in the sea and maybe even an octopus. But we must hurry," said Nikos.

Before long Linus was staring, wide-eyed, at the fish market. Hundreds of people were carrying fish, smelling fish, and poking fish with their fingers. Some fish were so large that two men could barely carry them.

Some were so small that a hundred fit in a handbasket.

Most of the fish went to small food stands. Few Romans had kitchens at home. Almost everyone in Rome bought meals cooked at food stands.

Nikos and Linus left the fish market and moved on to the meat, grain, oil, wine, and spice markets. Linus saw how Rome brought food to the one million or so people who lived there. By the end of the day, he knew he had learned some very important things. He also knew he was very hungry.

A Busy City

Lucia and her grandfather climbed the white marble steps of the Temple of Jupiter. A huge gold statue of Jupiter, king of the gods, looked down on them as they entered.

Grandfather stopped to speak to another senator. Lucia waited on the steps of the temple. She looked out over the city. Rome was so big! The people looked tiny as they walked among the great buildings and forums.

Lucia turned her eyes on the Forum of Rome, the city's oldest forum.

Thousands of people were talking and shouting, buying and selling, walking, running, and standing still. The Forum was like the city—filled with noise and excitement and people.

Lucia and Grandfather walked all through Rome that day. They visited temples and theaters. They ate at food stands and drank from the fountains.

Grandfather pointed out people from every province: Egyptians, Greeks, redheaded people from Gaul, and dark-skinned people from Africa.

Lucia was happy to be part of this noisy, crowded, exciting city. There was so much to see and to learn.

"Grandfather, will you take me again tomorrow? Please? I want to know more of our city. I am so proud to be a Roman!"

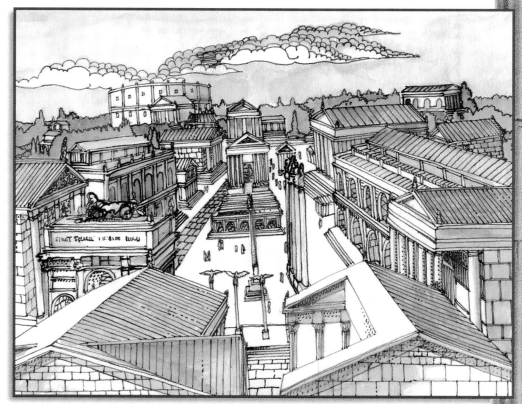

The Forum of Rome was a grand collection of buildings, as shown in this drawing.

Linus Gets Lost "It appears my grandson has a poor memory," said Grandfather. "I remember telling him not to go into the underground passageway, and that is exactly where he has gone."

Lucia started down the passageway to the underground part of the Colosseum. She thought maybe she could help find Linus, even though she did not like the look of the dark passageway.

Grandfather called her back. "No, Lucia. Don't you go looking for your brother," he said. "I will speak to the commander of the sailors. We may need some help to find him down there. Until we get some help, Linus can learn just how lost he can get down there. Perhaps it will help his poor memory."

Grandfather turned to Nikos. "Nikos, tell the commander of the sailors I want to see him after the **awning** is in place."

Nikos began climbing the hundreds of steps to the top of the Colosseum. The senator took Lucia's hand and led her onto the sunlit floor of the Colosseum.

"Lucia, I want you to understand how they built this great arena," said Grandfather. "It is the finest in Rome, and it has seating for 50,000 people.

> **vocabulary**
> **awning** a sheet of material used for protection from the sun or rain

"The round outside wall is built like an aqueduct, arches of stone stacked on each other. Arches also support the inside rows of seats, which look like a giant oval stairway.

"Look all around the very top of the arena. There are 1,000 sailors from the Roman navy up there. They are waiting for the command to roll out the awning. The awning is an immense canvas roof that shades the seats from the sun.

"There are many passageways under the floor of the arena. They connect dozens of rooms and chambers. Some of these rooms hold wild animals. Others are for the gladiators. One passageway connects the gladiator school to the arena. When it is time for a big gladiator fight, the gladiators are led out of one door, and the animals out of another."

Linus Meets the Gladiators

Linus was very sure of two things. He was very sure he was lost. And he was very sure that he wanted to get out of the underground passages.

He wasn't sure, but he thought he might have heard a low growling sound. It was a sound that a large animal might make.

Linus held his breath until he heard the sound again. This time it was louder—much louder. He was sure it was a very large animal.

Linus ran back down the dark passageway. He didn't know he could run so fast. He kept running until he saw a stairway. At the top of the stairway, he saw the sky.

A moment later, Linus was blinking at the bright sunlight in a sand-covered arena. He looked around and saw he was surrounded by fierce-looking warriors.

They were wearing helmets and carrying swords. They were covered with sweat and dust. They were looking at him.

Someone shouted, "Get that boy!"

Linus ran down the stairs and back into the dark passageway. He kept running.

Meanwhile, Lucia saw Nikos at the top of the Colosseum. He was delivering Grandfather's message to the naval commander. A moment later, the great awning began to unroll. Lucia felt better. Soon the sailors would be able to help find Linus, and she could stop worrying.

Suddenly, Linus ran through a doorway on the other side of the arena. He kept running until he reached his grandfather. He hugged him and would not let go. Linus was very pale.

"I'm glad you could join us, boy. We were just going to explore the underground chambers and visit the gladiator school," Grandfather teased.

This is a model of the Colosseum, as it would have looked in Linus's time.

The Chariot Races

Grandfather smiled and said, "Lucia, as much as I love this arena, I never come to the gladiator contests or the wild animal fights. I don't like killing, even though many Romans do. I'd rather watch the chariot races at the Circus Maximus."

"So would I, Grandfather," said Linus. "This place scares me. Could we leave here, please, right now?"

"We will wait here for Nikos," said Grandfather. "While we are waiting, you will think of a special way to thank Nikos for climbing to the top of the Colosseum to help find you. You will also apologize to your sister."

Grandfather signaled to Nikos and pointed to Linus. Nikos spoke to the commander. The naval commander saluted the senator. Nikos started the long walk back down.

Circus Maximus

On the way to the Circus Maximus, Nikos carried Linus on his shoulders, and Lucia held her grandfather's hand.

This artwork from about A.D. 300 shows gladiators fighting.

It was a beautiful day but the streets were almost empty.

"Where is everyone?" asked Lucia.

At that moment, a great roar filled the air. It was a lot like thunder. Another great roar sounded, even louder than the first one.

Grandfather laughed, "I'm certain that not everyone in Rome is in the Circus Maximus. But the Circus Maximus can seat 250,000 people. It is much larger than the Colosseum, with a huge oval racetrack. The chariot races are the most exciting show in Rome.

"They race twelve chariots, each pulled by four fast horses. The racetrack is a dangerous place. The drivers and the horses must be very well trained. Even so, terrible accidents can happen."

Grandfather looked at Nikos. "I'm afraid we must plan our trip to the races for another time. It seems that one of us has had enough excitement for today."

Linus was fast asleep on Nikos's shoulder.

Ruins   The Romans were expert builders. They built bridges, roads, aqueducts, and thousands of buildings all over the Roman world. A few of those ancient bridges are still in use today.

Many old roads and aqueducts are found in places once ruled by Rome. The remains of ancient buildings are also standing in Rome and other places. These remains are called *ruins*.

Most Roman ruins are about 2,000 years old. Because they are so old, these ruins are usually damaged.

Weather caused most of the damage to the Roman ruins. Heat, cold, rain, snow, hail, and wind all played a part. Earthquakes and fires have also harmed some of these ancient buildings.

Over many hundreds of years, people have taken pieces from old Roman buildings to use in other structures. The most recent damage has come from wars and air pollution.

When we look at a ruin, it is difficult to imagine what that building looked like in Roman times. However, there is an area in Italy where nature has actually protected and preserved these ancient buildings. This area is southeast of Rome, near the Bay of Naples and Mount Vesuvius.

Mount Vesuvius

Mount Vesuvius is a volcano. A volcano is formed when rock pushes up from deep underground.

This painting shows what the eruption of Mount Vesuvius may have looked like.

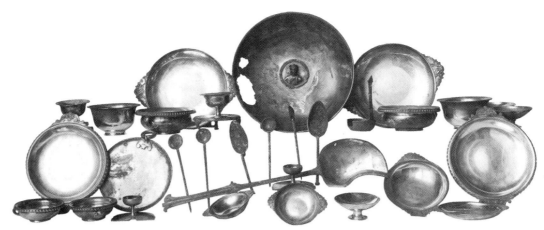

These dishes were dug up from the ruins of Pompeii.

This rock is so hot it is molten, or melted. Molten rock flows like liquid mud. When molten rock pushes through Earth's crust, it explodes in the air. Then it flows out on the surface of Earth. Later it cools and becomes rock hard. A volcano is a mountain of cooled molten rock.

Molten rock shoots out of a volcano during a volcanic eruption. Volcanic eruptions can destroy plant and animal life. Rock and hot ash explode in the air and fall around the volcano.

Sometimes volcanic eruptions throw enough smoke, dirt, and **debris** (deh BREE) into the sky to block the light of the sun. The area around the volcano may remain dark for several days, while the debris falls back to Earth.

Mount Vesuvius Buries Pompeii

Mount Vesuvius erupted on August 24, A.D. 79. Rock and ash exploded from the volcano and fell like rain for two days.

Six miles away from the volcano stood a town called Pompeii (pom PAY). Rock and ash from the eruption buried the entire town.

Pompeii disappeared under 23 feet of volcanic debris.

The weight of volcanic debris crushed the roof of every building in Pompeii. This caused damage to those buildings during the eruption. After the eruption, that same volcanic debris protected Pompeii. It remained buried and forgotten for almost 1,700 years.

Pompeii Is Found

The buried town was found again in 1763. Since then, people from all around the world have come to Pompeii. Some people came to find valuable statues or gold coins. Some people came to learn about Roman buildings. Others came to learn about volcanic eruptions. It took years of digging to find the answers about Pompeii.

Today more than half the town has been dug up. The digging continues, slowly and carefully so nothing will be damaged.

vocabulary
debris the pieces left of something after it has been destroyed

Daily Life in Pompeii

Much of what we know about the daily life of Roman people we have learned from Pompeii. The buildings of Pompeii are filled with things people used and looked at and enjoyed every day. These things help us to understand the people of ancient Rome.

About 20,000 people lived and worked in Pompeii. The town was built on the bank of a river that flowed into the Bay of Naples. Ships from all over the Roman world could trade at Pompeii.

The townspeople traded wine, olive oil, grain, pottery, and wool cloth. Pompeii had a busy marketplace in its forum. Farmers sold fruits and vegetables, while politicians made speeches and poets recited their latest poems.

Pompeii had more than 200 places to eat and drink. There were craftspeople who made metal cups and dishes, and shops that made and sold perfume. The town had bakers, builders, and bankers.

The People of Pompeii

The people of Pompeii loved art. Paintings were everywhere on the walls of shops and houses. Huge statues decorated the temples and the town forum. Beautiful **mosaics** covered the walls and floors of homes and public buildings.

The people of Pompeii also had fun. They kept dogs, caged birds, and beautiful gardens. They spent lazy afternoons in the beautiful public baths or the town swimming pool. They exercised and wrestled at the town gym. Pompeii had theaters for plays and concerts and an amphitheater for brutal gladiator fights.

The people of Pompeii drank from public fountains on street corners and wrote messages on walls of almost every building in the town. They had huge temples to their gods, but Venus—the goddess of love—seems to have been their favorite.

We know all of these things because Mount Vesuvius blew up about 2,000 years ago. The explosion was a disaster for the people who lived in Pompeii, but it has been a great thing for historians who want to know more about life in the ancient Roman Empire.

> **vocabulary**
> **mosaic** artwork made of many small pieces of colorful stone or tile

This room in a house in Pompeii had beautiful mosaic floors.

Luciano Is Embarrassed It was the year 2000, in modern Rome. The teacher looked around the classroom and began the lesson: "After he defeated Antony and Cleopatra, Octavian was the ruler of the Roman world."

"Octavian allowed the Roman Senate to name him Augustus. He also liked the title 'First Citizen of Rome.' He never allowed the senate to name him the king. But it did not really matter. The Roman republic was gone forever."

"Augustus was the first Roman emperor, even though he never admitted it. Emperors ruled in Rome for the next 500 years, and in Constantinople for 1,000 years after that."

Suddenly the teacher turned to one of the students and asked a question. "Luciano, who was Octavian?" All the students turned in their seats to look at Luciano (loo chee AH noh).

"I'm sorry," Luciano said, "I wasn't listening. I was looking out the window." Luciano was very embarrassed.

"I accept your apology, Luciano. You are honest. But I don't want my students to apologize; I want them to learn. Come up here near me and take a seat." Luciano picked up his book and quickly moved to his new seat.

"Tonight I want everyone to read about the early Roman emperors,—the ones who followed Augustus. Tomorrow we will talk about them. Luciano, please remain seated. The rest of you may go home now."

Roman emperors who won great victories were cheered as they were carried through Rome.

A Special Assignment

When the other students had gone, the teacher turned to Luciano and said, "Today was your last day as a student who looks out the window during class. Tomorrow is your first day as a student who participates in class. I will ask you to tell the class about the years of the great Roman peace, the Pax Romana. Be sure to read about this time in the early days of the Roman Empire tonight."

Luciano held his book under his arm as he walked home. The streets of Rome were crowded and noisy. He wondered if Rome had been this crowded during the time of emperors.

When Luciano got home, he looked in his book to find out about the great Roman peace. In a few moments he began to read. He was still reading when his mother called him to dinner.

The Great Roman Peace

The next day, Luciano took his seat in the classroom. The teacher looked at the class and said, "I've asked Luciano to tell us about the time of the great Roman peace. Please listen carefully."

Luciano stood up and said, "For the first 200 years, the Roman Empire was peaceful most of the time. The people of the Roman world were safe from civil war. The empire grew larger and wealthier than ever before.

"During this time, most of the emperors were wise and generous. Only a few were mean and selfish," he said.

"Thank you, Luciano. You have done well," said the teacher. Luciano was happy. He had really enjoyed reading about the history of his city. After school, the teacher said, "Tomorrow, I will ask you about the early Christians who lived during this time."

The Early Christians

The next day Luciano told the class, "The early Christians were people who followed the teachings of Jesus. They believed in one god. They also believed it was most important to live in God's kingdom after they died. The Romans did not like the idea of any kingdom being more important than Rome.

"The Christians respected the government and paid their taxes, but many Romans thought the Christians were dangerous to Rome. The Romans were always afraid of angering the gods. They wanted everyone in the empire to worship their own gods *and* the Roman gods too. This way, the Romans thought, no gods would get angry and punish the Romans.

"The Romans thought that the Christians were reckless. The Christians worshiped only one God. They would not worship other gods. The Romans thought the Christians were taking a chance of angering the other gods and getting the whole human race in trouble."

Some Christians, such as those shown praying here, were forced to face wild animals as punishment for their beliefs.

Persecution of the Christians

The teacher smiled brightly and said, "Thank you, Luciano. You have done a fine job again today."

The teacher turned to the class and said, "The Romans **persecuted** the Christians because of their religious beliefs. Whenever something bad happened in Rome, the Romans blamed the Christians.

"For example, there was a terrible fire in A.D. 64. Large areas of Rome were destroyed. The emperor Nero blamed the Christians, but Nero was a very selfish man. According to an old story, he cared so little about Rome that he strummed the strings of a musical instrument called a *lyre* while the city burned. Today we have an expression, 'fiddling while Rome burns.'

It means paying no attention to great disasters taking place around you.

"At times the Christians were treated as criminals. They were put in prison or killed for not worshiping the Roman gods. Sometimes Christians were made to face wild animals in the Colosseum.

"The Romans persecuted the Christians for many years. But the number of Christians continued to grow, even though it was dangerous to be Christian. This is because the Christians welcomed poor people and slaves. The Christians promised a better life in the next world for those who suffered in the Roman world."

vocabulary
persecute to treat people cruelly and unfairly

Luciano's Next Assignment   Luciano had begun to enjoy participating in class. Each day after school, the teacher gave him a special assignment. The following day, Luciano would tell the class about what he had read the night before.

Luciano thought about his new assignment as he walked home from school. The teacher had told him to report to the class about the time after the great Roman peace. This was the time the empire began to **decline.** Luciano wondered what had happened.

On his way home, Luciano walked across a beautiful old stone bridge. He knew the Romans built the bridge in ancient times.

vocabulary
decline to grow weaker

He thought about the millions of people who had walked across that bridge in the 2,000 years since it was new. Luciano felt very proud to be a Roman.

When he got home, Luciano told his mother about his special assignment. His mother was pleased. She wanted him to work hard and enjoy learning.

Luciano began his reading assignment. The teacher said he would find out about big changes in the empire.

The picture carved on this ancient stone shows a bridge much like the one Luciano walked across.

This legion of Roman soldiers was lead by a general, on the right.

Weak and Corrupt Emperors

The next day, Luciano told the class about some of the changes Rome experienced. "First, the hard-working, thoughtful emperors of the great Roman peace were gone. For the next 80 years, most of the emperors were greedy and selfish, like Nero."

The teacher stood up and said, "That is correct, Luciano. Those emperors did not work hard for the people. They also did a very poor job of protecting the provinces from attack. Protecting the provinces took a lot of time and cost a lot of money. The emperors preferred to spend that money for their own pleasure.

"The corrupt emperors named corrupt men to be generals in the army. Often an emperor would be killed by one of his generals, and then that general would become the new emperor.

The new emperor would then kill the family and all the friends of the old emperor. Sometimes there would be two or three emperors in a single year. This meant that lots of senators and other powerful Romans would be killed. For the old patrician families, life in Rome was very risky during this time.

"Often civil wars would start as generals battled one another to take over the empire. Many towns and farms were destroyed during the civil wars. These wars made trading very difficult. In some parts of the empire, people had very little food. In other parts, people lost their jobs and their homes. Throughout the empire, people often lived in fear."

The Barbarians Invade

The teacher now asked Luciano, "What other big changes happened during this time?"

Luciano replied, "The Roman army was also very different. The soldiers who had fought for the glory of Rome were gone. Romans no longer thought that serving in the army was a great honor. The Roman army had many soldiers who did not know about Rome at all. These soldiers lived in places that were very far from Rome, often the most distant parts of the Empire. The Romans called these people *barbarians.*

The Romans thought the barbarians were very uncivilized, but they allowed them to serve in the Roman army."

"Very good, Luciano. Those were very important changes in the Roman army," said the teacher. "Many barbarian tribes lived along the borders of the Roman Empire. Sometimes large armies of barbarians invaded Roman provinces."

"Rome's armies might be fighting barbarian invaders and fighting a civil war among themselves at the same time. Many of Rome's best soldiers died fighting against other Romans."

Rome's Army Grows Weak

"During this time, Rome's leaders treated the army very poorly. Soldiers often had to wait for months or even years for their pay to come from Rome. Without money to buy food, the soldiers had to steal food to live. Many Roman soldiers lived by **pillaging** nearby farms and towns."

"Gradually the Roman army became weak and dishonest, just like the rest of the Roman government.

"As the Roman army grew weaker, the barbarian armies grew stronger.

They forced the Romans out of large areas in the western and northern parts of the empire. Before long, the Roman Empire was ready to **collapse.**"

vocabulary
pillage to steal things using force and violence
collapse to fall down suddenly

Diocletian

The teacher continued. "Just before all was lost, a strong, thoughtful man named Diocletian (dye oh KLEE shun) became emperor. He began by defeating a fierce barbarian army. He also made another major change. Luciano, can you tell us about this change?"

Luciano was on his feet at once. He spoke in a clear voice, "Diocletian changed the whole Roman government. He ordered that instead of one emperor, the Roman world would have two emperors. One would govern the west and one the east. Diocletian named honest, hardworking men to rule the empire with him. He made many more changes in the government. After he ruled for 20 years, he did something no emperor had ever done. He gave up his job and retired."

This coin shows the emperor Diocletian wearing a laurel wreath. He ruled between A.D. 284 and A.D. 305.

Luciano's Last Assignment Luciano had glanced ahead in his textbook, so he knew the story of the Roman Empire was nearly over. He felt a little bit sad because this story would always be very special to him.

While studying the story of the Roman Empire, Luciano had discovered how much he enjoyed learning and talking in class.

This time, the teacher gave him an assignment to read about Emperor Constantine and the city of Constantinople. Luciano was very curious. He hurried home to begin his reading.

Constantine Takes Control

The next day, the teacher began, "After Diocletian retired, the Roman Empire struggled through almost 20 years of civil wars. Finally, a strong leader took control of the empire. His name was Constantine.

"Constantine followed the example of Diocletian. He named honest men to help him rule the empire. But Constantine also did something Diocletian had refused to do: He allowed Christians to practice their religion without persecution. In fact, Constantine actively supported the Christian religion. He is remembered as the first Christian emperor.

"After Constantine ruled the Roman Empire for a while, he decided to move the government from Rome."

The teacher turned to Luciano and asked, "Luciano, would you tell us where Constantine moved the government?"

This mosaic shows Constantine holding a model of Constantinople.

The emperor Justinian had a Christian church called Hagia Sophia built in Constantinople, which is now called Istanbul.

Constantinople

Luciano had prepared a little report. "In A.D. 330," he said, "Constantine moved the government of the Roman Empire to a city in the eastern part of the empire called Byzantium. Byzantium was an old city with a great big racetrack like the Circus Maximus in Rome.

"Constantine thought that Byzantium should have a new name. He decided to name the city after himself. So Byzantium became Constantinople.

"But you won't find Constantinople on maps today," Luciano continued, "because the city's name has changed again. Now it's called Istanbul, and it's in the country of Turkey."

"Thank you, Luciano," said the teacher. "You did very well."

The Byzantine Empire

The teacher continued, "Constantine ruled from Constantinople for several years before he died. After his death, there were more civil wars, and the western part of the Roman Empire was eventually separated from the eastern part. This meant that there were two empires instead of one empire with two rulers.

"The Eastern Empire included Constantinople—the ancient city of Byzantium. So it became known as the Byzantine Empire. The Byzantine Empire remained powerful and lasted for more than 1,000 years.

"Constantinople was one of the most important cities in the world. In Constantinople there were traders and travelers from Asia, Africa, and Europe. Philosophers discussed important ideas and artists blended Greek, Roman, and Middle Eastern styles to create beautiful mosaics and other works of art.

"The Eastern Empire was ruled by a series of emperors. One of the most famous of these emperors was named Justinian. Justinian built a beautiful Christian church called Hagia Sophia (HAH jah so FEE uh). He also worked to improve the laws of the Byzantine Empire.

"Although Justinian ruled the Eastern Empire, many miles from Rome, he knew that his empire had been built by Romans and was governed by Roman laws. Justinian wanted the people of his empire to **preserve** the old laws of the Romans, so he collected all the old Roman laws and had them written down. This collection of Roman laws was known as the Justinian Code."

> **vocabulary**
> **preserve** to keep or save
> **sack** to steal and destroy things in a city that has been defeated by an army

The Western Empire

The teacher continued, "The Western Empire didn't do as well as the Eastern Empire. In fact, by the time Justinian became emperor in the east, the Western Empire had completely collapsed.

"The Western Empire was less wealthy than the Eastern Empire, and it was surrounded by warlike neighbors. Barbarian tribes often attacked the borders of the Western Empire. As the years went by, these barbarians conquered more and more land. The armies of the Western Empire could not stop them. Eventually the barbarians **sacked** the city of Rome.

"The Western Empire struggled against the barbarians for another 60 years. Finally, in A.D. 476, a barbarian leader forced the emperor of the Western Empire to surrender and give up his throne. That was the end of the Western Empire.

"We have reached the end of our lessons on the Romans," said the teacher. "Now I think we should say thank you to another person for his important work in helping us to know and understand the Romans. Thank you, Luciano. We are very proud of you."

The students clapped and cheered.

Glossary

awning a sheet of material used for protection from the sun or rain

barge a boat with a flat bottom, usually used for carrying goods

civil war a war between people who live in the same country

collapse to fall down suddenly

conquer to win control of a land by attacking an enemy or fighting a war

consul the most important official in the Roman republic

debris the pieces left of something after it has been destroyed

decline to grow weaker

legend an old, well-known story, usually more entertaining than truthful

legion a unit or group of soldiers

mosaic artwork made of many small pieces of colorful stone or tile

peninsula a piece of land sticking out into a body of water

persecute to treat people cruelly and unfairly

pillage to steal things using force and violence

pillar a tall, solid support post

preserve to keep or save

province an area under the control of a faraway government

sack to steal and destroy things in a city that has been defeated by an army

symbol a picture or object that is a sign for something; for example, the American flag is a symbol of the United States

toga a loose robe worn by citizens of ancient Rome

virtue goodness

47

CREDITS

All photographs © Pearson Learning unless otherwise noted.

PHOTOS:
Cover:
Frgd: Bettmann/Corbis. *Bkgd:* Stone
Interior:
1: SuperStock, Inc. 2: Leeds Museum and Art Galleries (city museum) UK/The Bridgeman Art Library. 4–5: Blair, Elizabeth Hunter/The Bridgeman Art Library. 5: Early Roman bronze coin, ca. B.C. 350 Gift of Mrs. James P. Tolman. Courtesy of Museum of Fine Arts, Boston. 8: Gianni Dagli Orti/Corbis. 9: Dagli Orti/Museo Prenestino Palestrina/The Art Archive/The Picture Desk. 10–11: Massimo/Corbis. 12: Gustavo Tomsich/Corbis. 13: Dagli Orti/Museo della Civilta Romania, Rome/The Art Archive/The Picture Desk. 14: The Berger Collection at the Denver Art Museum USA/The Bridgeman Art Library. 15: The Art Archive/The Picture Desk. 16: Gianni Dagli Orti/Corbis. 17: Bettmann/Corbis. 18: The Picture Desk. 19: Archivo Iconografico, SA/Corbis. 20: Araldo de Luca/Corbis. 21: Bettmann/Corbis. 22: Kea Publishing Services Ltd./Corbis. 24: Lawrence Manning/Corbis. 25: James L. Amos/Corbis. 28: Bettmann/Corbis. 29: The Bridgeman Art Library. 30: Historical Picture Archive/Corbis. 33: Dorling Kindersley Picture Library. 34: Archivo Iconografico, SA/Corbis. 35: Gianni Dagli Orti/Corbis. 37: Mimmo Jodice/Corbis. 38: Mary Evans Picture Library. 40: Bettmann/Corbis. 41: Scala/Art Resource. 42: Rob Shone/Dorling Kindersley Picture Library. 43, 44: The Bridgeman Art Library. 45: Kea Publishing Services Ltd./Corbis.

Illustration: 27, Joel Iskowitz

Maps: 3,10, 23: Mapping Specialists, Ltd.

Border Art: Dorothea Fox and Cathy Pawlowski

Initial Capital Art: Cathy Pawlowski